To SBG

Prologue

My legs felt heavy as I strolled over to the restaurant along with my husband. I felt bad, really bad that I had to drag him to this meeting.

Finally, I spotted her in a corner and the grimace on my face turned into a dazzling smile. I waved enthusiastically. She is my mother after all. No matter how she makes me feel.

I settled casually into the seat opposite her, asking about her day. She lapsed instantly into a long ramble of her neighbors' arguments, being bullied by her relatives (as always) and being suppressed by her own husband. I nodded slowly and frequently to her monologue, no matter how many times I have heard it. My husband dazed off into a distant land.

The food came, and I told her about my new job. It was an extremely good opportunity, but I had to settle for lower pay due to my lack of experience. I gushed about how it's a one-of-a-kind opportunity and how jealous my friends are. She grimaced and started rubbing her temples. "Why did you let go of such a good paying job? There are many people who are poor and are queuing to be in your shoes. You mustn't let your interests distract you. You must focus on success. Then I can be proud of you. People are looking at us, jeering at our failures. You mustn't let them be right."

I nodded and finished the rest of my meal in silence. My husband nudged me to leave soon, jabbing his fingers at his watch. I kicked him and glared. This is my mother, I mouthed.

We soon completed the meals and stood to leave. She was deeply concentrated on commenting how my sisters were not giving her income and were useless as her kids. As she entered the station, I smiled and asked her to take care, and that we will see her soon.

My husband turned towards me and asked, doesn't she know you are pregnant?

I faced him and said "Yes. She just didn't ask."

-   Janice

Toxic people can be anyone around you. Do not let them dictate your lives.

\-   Sean Cox

Contents

Who Can Be The Toxic Person In Your Life?

- **Your Best Friend:** This is a person who you have known until the end of time. Possibly you went to grade school together or you were neighbors growing up. Presently you feel regretful about the closure of the relationship.

- **Your Relative:** This is a person who comes as a bundle with another person in your life. Possibly it's your accomplice's significant other or your companion's sibling who dependably follows along, or your closest companion's childhood sweetheart. You feel regretful in light of the fact that you would prefer not to put your person in a clumsy circumstance.

- **Your Colleague:** This is a person who you see all the time in a particular aspect of your life. Somebody you work with consistently. Somebody on your banner football group. Somebody who lives over the lobby. You feel regretful about getting over them since you see them all the dang time.

- **Your Family:** You may never realize you have this person around by any stretch of the imagination!

Types Of Toxic People And How To Spot Them

The Non-Stop Blabber

Have you at any point been conversing with somebody who continues intruding on you? Perhaps I should overhaul that sentence: have you at any point been trying to converse with somebody who won't give you a chance to get a word in? Conversational narcissists LOVE to discuss themselves—or simply hear themselves talk. They don't put forth any inquiries, they don't sit tight for your reactions and they won't quiet down. In a relationship, these persons will wind up being totally conceited and never be mindful of your requirements.

I Am Always Right

This is somebody who needs to control everything and everybody around them. They need to be responsible for what you do, what you say, and even what you think. You know the person I am talking about– they go crazy when you can't help contradicting them and won't quit trying to persuade you that they are correct and you ought to do what they say. In a relationship, this person will give you no breathing room and always will bother you to the point that you are in total arrangement with them. Be watchful, these persons will pursue your passionate, conversational and mental flexibility until the point that you don't have anything cleared out. Get out while you can!

The Dementor

A dementor is also known as a profound vampire since they tend to drain the energy out of you or drain you sincerely dry. These are the sorts of persons who dependably have something pitiful, negative or skeptical to state. In discussions and connections, they never can see the positive and have a tendency to carry everybody down with them. In case you're with somebody and they just have awful things to state at whatever point you see them, keep an eye out, it probably won't beat that.

The Kardashian

Some toxic persons are magnets for drama. Something definitely isn't right. Continuously. What's more, obviously, once an issue is unraveled, another develops. Furthermore, they just need your compassion, sensitivity, and support– however not your recommendation! You offer assistance and arrangements, yet they never appear to need to settle anything. Rather, they grumble and whine. In a relationship, dramatization magnets are casualties and flourish in an emergency since it makes them feel vital. On the off chance that somebody is a signal for difficulty, keep an eye out, you may one day turn out to be a piece of the show.

The Gossip Monger

My companions and I can detect a gossip monger from a mile away and I need to demonstrate to you best practices to too. A gossip monger is an envious judgmental person. Desirous persons are unbelievably toxic in light of the fact that they have so much interior self-loathing that they can't be glad for anybody around them. Furthermore, normally, their envy turns out as judgment, feedback or babble. As indicated by them, every other person is terrible, uncool or ailing somehow. On the off chance that somebody begins desirously tattling with you about other persons, keep an eye out. This may be a harmful person—and no one can really tell what they say in regards to you in the face of your good faith.

The Liar

I met various liars. it's depleting to have a toxic swindler in your life. Regardless of whether they tell little deceptions or significant falsehoods, it's difficult to confide in a liar in a relationship. Unscrupulousness channels us since we always are questioning their words. In the event that your instinct is ringing alerts, at that point keep an eye out, get out before you're deceived.

Why Are You So Dumb?

This person pounds everything in its way. He is in every case right, doesn't consider any other person's sentiments or thoughts, and always puts themselves first. In a relationship, tanks are unfathomably haughty and see their genuine beliefs as certainties. This is on the grounds that they frequently think they are the sharpest person in the room. Thus, they see each discussion and person as a test that must be prevailed upon. They once in a while consider others to be equivalents—and this can be tested when attempting to frame a cherishing association. On the off chance that you feel your thoughts are being kept running over, or you are not being regarded, get out while despite everything you can!

Checklist Of Toxic People. Are You One?

Dealing with such a person can be difficult and draining, to say the least. But you might never realize it. In fact, it may challenge what you know about yourself and push you to the limits. Here are some traits to familiarize yourself with, and to help you navigate these trying relationships. Tick as many as possible to see if you have one in your life!

Manipulative	Inspire persons to do what they need them to do. It's about them. They utilize other persons to achieve whatever their objective happens to be.	
Judgmental	Keep your eyes and ears open for feedback—about you, what you've done, and what you didn't do. It's never about them, and they will lie on the off chance that it serves them.	
Take no responsibility for their feelings	Their emotions are anticipated onto you. In the event that you attempt to direct this out toward them, they will probably fervently protect their point of view and assume no liability for nearly anything they do.	
The victim status	They don't perceive any motivation to, in light of the fact that things are dependably another person's blame. They attempt to pick up sensitivity and consideration by asserting "casualty" status.	
Inconsistent	It's difficult to know who you're with at some random time since they are regularly not a similar person. They may change their point of view, demeanor, and conduct contingent upon what they believe they have to achieve or what they need to have occurred, and they know how to be caring when they need something from you.	
"You must save me (and not them) if I	Influence you to pick them over another person, or something they need over something you need.	

fall into the water"	Regularly, this transforms into a "gap and overcome" dynamic in which the main decision is them, even to the point of expecting you to slice off other important connections to fulfill them.	
Makes you defensive	They're not inspired by your perspective or trys. They are preeminent controllers: their strategies may incorporate being ambiguous and discretionary, and additionally redirecting the focal point of the dialog to how you're talking about an issue. They center around issues, not arrangements.	
Not caring, supportive, or interested in happening to you	It's always about them. Beware of people who find fault with you and make you wrong. Loyalty is foreign to them.	
The drama king/queen	Everything transpires. What they truly need is your continuous sensitivity and support, and they will make one dramatization after another with a specific end goal to get it. "settling" and "sparing" them never works, particularly since you most likely consideration more about the end result for them than they do.	
Leaves you emotionally drained	Time with them is tied in with dealing with their business, which will abandon you feeling disappointed and unfulfilled, if not furious.	
Narcissistic	They request your full focus and try to persuade you that you have to join their camp. They're correct; you're off-base. What's more, you have to do what they say.	

I Am Tired. What Should I Do?

Did someone pop into your head as you read this book?

Difficult people are drawn to the reasonable ones and all of us have likely had (or have) at least one person in our lives who have us bending around ourselves like barbed wire in endless attempts to please them – only to never really get there.

Their damage lies in their subtlety and the way they can engender that classic response, 'It's not them, it's me.' They can have you questioning your 'over-reactiveness', your 'oversensitivity', your 'tendency to misinterpret'. If you're the one who's continually hurt or the one who is constantly adjusting your own behavior to avoid being hurt, then chances are that it's not you and it's very much them.

Being able to spot their harmful behavior is the first step to minimizing their impact. You might not be able to change what they do, but you can change what you do with it, and any idea that toxic somebody in your life might have that they can get away with it.

Now that you have identified the person, you may realize that most often than not, this person has been in your life for some time. But why are you still hanging around him/her?

Here's the problem: Guilt

Well, you deserve to have wonderful, supportive and loving people in your life. In fact, life is too short to spend time with people who don't help you be your best self.

So how do you immunize yourself against toxic people?

Stop trying to please them

Toxic persons made sense of quite a while back that conventional persons will go to uncommon lengths to keep the general population they care about upbeat. On the off chance that your trys to please aren't working or aren't going on for long, perhaps it's a great opportunity to stop. Leave and return when the state of mind has moved. You are not in charge of any other person's sentiments. On the off chance that you have accomplished something unconsciously to hurt someone, ask, discuss it and if require be, apologize. At any rate, you shouldn't need to figure.

You don't owe anybody anything

If it doesn't feel like a favor, it's not.

Be really clear on what's yours and what's theirs

You'll wind up legitimizing and protecting and frequently this will go around in circles – in light of the fact that it's not about you. On the off chance that you feel just as you're safeguarding yourself too often against allegations or inquiries that don't fit, you may be anticipated on to. You don't need to clarify, legitimize or safeguard yourself or manage a failed allegation. Keep in mind that.

Enough will never be enough

Few things are fatal – unless it's life or death, chances are it can wait.

Just move forward – without them

Persons don't need to apologize to not be right. Also, you needn't bother with a conciliatory sentiment to push ahead. Try not to surrender your fact, however, don't prop the contention up. There's simply no point. A few people need to be correct more than they need to be cheerful and you have preferred activities over to give feed to one side contenders.

You don't need their approval

Don't let them dampen you or shrink you down to their size. You don't need their approval anyway – or anyone else's for that matter.

Know who cares

Persons who care about you won't let you continue feeling junk without trying to deal with it. That doesn't mean you'll deal with it obviously, yet in any event, they'll attempt. Accept it as an indication of their interest in the relationship on the off chance that they abandon you 'out there' for protracted sessions.

Don't buy into the argument

It's difficult to guard yourself against this type of control. Harmful persons have a method for drawing on the one time you didn't or the one time you did as confirmation of your inadequacies. You won't win. What's more, you don't have to.

Nobody has the right to stand in judgment

We're altogether permitted to fail to understand the situation every so often, however except if we've accomplished something that influences them no one has the privilege to remain in judgment. A few people can't be satisfied and a few people won't be beneficial for you – and ordinarily, that will have nothing to do with you. You can simply say no to superfluous insane. Be certain and claim your own shortcomings, your peculiarities and the things that make you sparkle. You needn't bother with anybody's endorsement, however, recollect in the event that somebody is striving to control, this is on the grounds that most likely on the grounds that they require yours. You don't generally need to give it yet on the off chance that you do, don't give the cost a chance to be too high.

So How Do Emotionally Intelligent People Handle Toxic People?

Toxic persons make no sense. Some are willfully ignorant of the antagonistic effect that they have on everyone around them, and others appear to get fulfillment from making bedlam and pushing other persons' catches. In any case, they make pointless intricacy, struggle, and most noticeably awful of all pressure.

Studies have long demonstrated that pressure can have an enduring, negative effect on the mind. Introduction to even a couple of long stretches of pressure bargains the viability of neurons in the hippocampus—a critical cerebrum region in charge of thinking and memory. Long stretches of pressure cause reversible harm to neuronal dendrites (the little "arms" that cerebrum cells use to speak with one another), and long stretches of pressure can forever pulverize neurons. Stress is an imposing danger to your prosperity—when worry gains of power, your cerebrum and your execution endure.

Most wellsprings of worry at work are anything but difficult to recognize. On the off chance that your non-benefit is attempting to arrive a give that your association needs to work, will undoubtedly feel pressure and likely know how to oversee it. It's the sudden wellsprings of stress that shock you and mischief you the most.

Ongoing exploration from the Department of Biological and Clinical Psychology at Friedrich Schiller University in Germany found that introduction to boosts that reason solid adverse feelings—a similar sort of presentation you get when managing harmful persons—made subjects' brains have a gigantic pressure reaction. Regardless of whether it's pessimism, savagery, the casualty disorder, or out and out insanity, harmful persons drive your mind into an endless spiral that ought to be dodged no matter what.

The capacity to deal with your feelings and to avoid panicking under stress has an immediate connection to your life. TalentSmart has led investigate with in excess of a million people, and they found that 90% of best entertainers are gifted at dealing with their feelings in the midst of worry so as to keep quiet and in charge. One of their most noteworthy blessings is the capacity to kill toxic persons. Top entertainers have all around sharpened adapting systems that they utilize to keep toxic persons under control.

To manage toxic persons viably, you require a methodology that empowers you, no matter how you look at it, to control what you can and dispense with what you can't. The vital thing to recall is that you are responsible for much more than you understand.

They Set Limits

Whiners and pessimistic persons are awful news since they flounder in their issues and neglect to center around arrangements. They need persons to join their pity party with the goal that they can rest easy thinking about themselves. Persons regularly feel strain to tune in to grumblers since they would prefer not to be viewed as hard or discourteous, however, there's a scarce difference between listening attentively and getting sucked into their negative enthusiastic winding.

You can evade this just by setting limits and removing yourself when vital. Consider it thusly: if the grumbler were smoking, okay stay there throughout the evening breathing in the second-hand smoke? You'd separate yourself, and you ought to do likewise with whiners. An incredible method as far as possible is to ask grumblers how they plan to settle the issue. They will either calm down or divert the discussion in a profitable way.

They Don't Die in the Fight

Successful people know how important it is to live to fight another day, especially when your foe is a toxic person. In conflict, unchecked emotion makes you dig your heels in and fight the kind of battle that can leave you severely damaged. When you read and respond to your emotions, you're able to choose your battles wisely and only stand your ground when the time is right.

They Rise Above

Toxic persons make you insane on the grounds that their conduct is so nonsensical. No doubt about it; their conduct genuinely conflicts with reason. So for what reason do you enable yourself to react to them candidly and get sucked in with the general mish-mash?

The more ridiculous somebody is, the less demanding it ought to be for you to expel yourself from their traps. Stop trying to beat them unexpectedly. Separation yourself from them candidly and approach your associations like they're a contextual analysis. You don't have to react to the enthusiastic turmoil—just the realities.

They Stay Aware of Their Emotions

Keeping up a passionate separation requires mindfulness. You can't prevent somebody from pushing your catches in the event that you don't perceive when it's occurring. Some of the time you'll wind up in circumstances where you'll have to regroup and pick the most ideal route forward. This is fine and you shouldn't be hesitant to get yourself some an opportunity to do as such. When you end up with an associate who is occupied with wrecked reasoning, now and then it's best to simply grin and gesture. In case you will need to fix them, it's smarter to give yourself some an opportunity to design the most ideal approach.

They Establish Boundaries

This is where a great many people tend to undercut themselves. They feel like since they work or live with somebody, they have no real way to control the disarray. This couldn't possibly be more off-base. Once you've discovered your approach to rising Above a man, you'll start to discover their conduct more unsurprising and less demanding to get it. This will prepare you to contemplate when and where you need to endure them and when you don't. For instance, regardless of whether you work with somebody nearly on a venture group, that doesn't imply that you need a similar level of one-on-one communication with them that you have with other colleagues.

You can set up a limit, yet you'll need to do as such intentionally and proactively. In the event that you let things happen normally, you will undoubtedly wind up continually involved in troublesome discussions. In the event that you set limits and choose when and where you'll connect with a troublesome person, you can control a significant part of the disarray. The main trap is to adhere to your weapons and keep limits set up when the person trys to infringe upon them, which they will.

They Won't Let Anyone Limit Their Joy

At the point when your feeling of joy and fulfillment are obtained through others, you are no longer the ace of your own satisfaction. At the point when candidly smart persons like something that they've done, they won't let anybody's conclusions or scornful comments remove that from them.

While it's difficult to kill your responses to what others consider you, you don't need to contrast yourself with others, and you can simply take persons' feelings with a grain of salt. That way, regardless of what toxic persons are considering or doing, your self-esteem originates from inside. Despite what persons consider you at a specific minute, one thing is sure—you're never as great or awful as is commonly said you seem to be.

They Don't Focus on Problems—Only Solutions

Where you concentrate decides your passionate state. When you focus on the issues you're confronting, you make and draw out negative feelings and stress. When you center around activities to better yourself and your conditions, you make a feeling of person viability that produces positive feelings and decreases pressure.

With regards to toxic persons, focusing on how insane and troublesome they are giving them control over you. Stop pondering how disturbing your troublesome person is, and center rather around how you will approach taking care of them. This makes you more successful by placing you in charge, and it will decrease the measure of pressure you encounter while cooperating with them.

They Don't Forget

Emotionally intelligent people are quick to forgive, but that doesn't mean that they forget. Forgiveness requires letting go of what's happened so that you can move on. It doesn't mean you'll give a wrongdoer another chance. Successful people are unwilling to be bogged down unnecessarily by others' mistakes, so they let them go quickly and are assertive in protecting themselves from future harm.

They Squash Negative Self-Talk

Now and again you retain the antagonism of other persons. There's nothing amiss with feeling terrible about how somebody is treating you, yet your self-talk (the considerations you have about your emotions) can either increase the pessimism or help you move past it. Negative self-talk is implausible, superfluous, and pointless. It sends you into a descending enthusiastic winding that is hard to haul out of. You ought to stay away from negative self-talk no matter what.

They Limit Their Caffeine Intake

Well, I don't really agree with this, but studies showed that drinking caffeine triggers the release of adrenaline. Adrenaline is the source of the "fight-or-flight" response, a survival mechanism that forces you to stand up and fight or run for the hills when faced with a threat. The fight-or-flight mechanism sidesteps rational thinking in favor of a faster response. This is great when a bear is chasing you, but not so great when you're surprised in the hallway by an angry coworker.

They Get Some Sleep

I can't emphasize enough about the importance of sleep to increasing your emotional intelligence and managing your stress levels. When you sleep, your brain literally recharges, shuffling through the day's memories and storing or discarding them (which causes dreams), so that you wake up alert and clear-headed. Your self-control, attention, and memory are all reduced when you don't get enough—or the right kind—of sleep. Sleep deprivation raises stress hormone levels on its own, even without a stressor present.

A good night's sleep makes you more positive, creative, and proactive in your approach to toxic people, giving you the perspective you need to deal effectively with them. It is also the miracle medicine of depression.

They Use Their Support System

It's enticing, yet altogether insufficient, to try to handle everything without anyone else's input. Everybody has somebody at work and additionally outside work who is on their group, pulling for them, and prepared to enable them to get the best from a troublesome circumstance. Distinguish these people throughout your life and attempt to look for their understanding and help when you require it. Something as basic as clarifying the circumstance can prompt another point of view. More often than not, other persons can see an answer that you can't on the grounds that they are not as sincerely put resources into the circumstance.

How To Cut Toxic People Out Of Your Life

So… what if all of the above doesn't work?

All things considered, there's an old fantasy that frogs will pull down different frogs attempting to get away from a pot of bubbling water. That is likely the stuff of legends, yet the dynamic is genuine: In everybody's life, there will dependably be persons who will oppose, undermine and attack the likelihood of personal growth.

This group of toxic people — whom we can call as "harmful" — may dislike your advancement for any number of reasons. Maybe they think you'll never again be a major part of their life on the off chance that you enhance excessively. Possibly they feel like your change uncovered their own particular deficiencies. Or then again maybe they're simply debilitated by the change.

The causes are less essential than the impacts, which can appear as outrage, disdain, disappointment, control or cold-bloodedness (or an incapacitating mix thereof). At some random minute, you may wind up managing harmful companions, relatives or associates who — intentionally or unwittingly — are subverting your bliss and development. Distinguishing these people and seeing how to oversee them is completely essential to your prosperity, achievement, and bliss.

Perhaps then, the fastest way is to avoid having such people in your life. Because in a very real way, your future depends on it.

What should I take note of?

Of course, tolerance for toxicity is relative to each person — you have to decide when someone requires distance and when they need to be cut out of your life. Those lines vary from person to person. For example, your sister will probably get more leeway than a coworker, but everyone's sister and coworkers are different, and everyone has a different threshold.

What we're discussing here is genuine toxic quality — the kind that taints, metastasizes, and assumes control over your life. Here are a couple of great indications of toxic persons.

It's uncommon for these harmful people to thoroughly attack your attempts at personal growth, however, it happens. In any event, they will positively back off your advancement. More to the point, okay need somebody in your life who's effectively contradicted to improving your life?

The appropriate response, obviously, is no. But that can be difficult to acknowledge until the point that you start to perceive the impacts of toxicity inside you.

Affected by a toxic person, you may second figure yourself on a vital choice. You may feel dismal, awkward and absolute embarrassed about your own advancement and prosperity. You may even the interpretation of a portion of the same toxic characteristics you disdain in others — something that happens to potentially anyone — on the grounds that harmful persons have an impossible to miss method for making you toxic yourself.

What's more, a greater amount of than not, the example occurs without us notwithstanding figuring it out. On the off chance that you've at any point had a harmful manager, at that point you know how this functions: His conduct makes you bad-tempered and severe, so you lose your temper with the group working under you, which makes your representatives turn out to be progressively troublesome with each other, which makes them convey that state of mind home to their loved ones, and before you know it, the toxic substance has unwittingly spread.

That is the manner by which danger works. It's infectious and tricky, even in kind, balanced persons. That is the thing that makes it so risky, and that is the reason for expelling toxic persons from your life is so basic.

First, a quick warning: Cutting toxic people out of your life can blow up in your face. That's part of the disease. With that said, it's absolutely crucial to remove these people from your life in a healthy and rational way.

So how do you go about removing these toxic people from your life and reclaiming the time and energy you've been giving them?

- **Accept that it might be a process.** Disposing of toxic components isn't in every case simple. They don't regard your limits presently, so it's possible they won't regard them later. They may return even after you instruct them to leave. You may need to instruct them to leave a few times previously they at last do. So remember that removing yourself is a continuous procedure.

- **Don't feel like you owe them a huge explanation.** Any clarifying you do is more for you than for them. Once more, reveal to them how you feel, which is a subject not open for banter. Or then again, in the event that you incline toward, keep it straightforward: Tell them smoothly and benevolent that you don't need them in your life any longer, and abandon it at that. How much or how little you let them know is truly up to you. Each relationship requires an alternate methodology.

- **Talk to them in a public place.** It's not inconceivable for toxic persons to get aggressive or even savage. Conversing with them openly can essentially lessen the odds of this incident. On the off chance that you keep running into issues, you can simply get up and take off.

- **Block them on social media.** If you have to do this, you are probably still highly affected by them. But do it if you cannot stop them from invading your space. Technology makes distancing more difficult, so don't leave any window open for them to bully or cajole you. You've set boundaries. Stick to them. This includes preventing them from contacting you via social media, if appropriate. Shutting down email and other lines of communication with a toxic person might also be in order.

- **Don't argue — just restate your boundaries.** It's enticing to fall into the dynamic of toxic quality by belligerence or battling — that is absolutely what harmful persons do. In the occasion they do return, make a guarantee with yourself to maintain a strategic distance from a contention. Immovably rehash your limits, at that point end correspondence. You're not attempting to "banter" the person into disregarding you. This isn't a transaction. You can, in any case, make it less and less appealing for them to continue pestering you. "Try not to nourish the trolls!"

- **Consider writing a letter.** Writing yourself a letter is a kind of dress practice for an in-person discussion. You're elucidating your considerations and articulating your emotions. You can likewise allude back to the letter later in the event that you have to recall why you settled on the choice to remove somebody. Since toxic persons regularly do all that they can to remain in your life, you'll require all the assistance you can get.

- **Consider creating distance instead of separation.** Keep in mind the person we discussed above — the person who's not toxic, but rather only a drag? You don't need to remove these persons of your life totally. You simply need to make remove by involving your opportunity with different companions and exercises and concurring not to encourage into their dynamic.

And in many cases, you might not have to "do" anything at all.

For some harmful connections — particularly with companions and associates — you'll just need to settle on an inward choice to make some space, without having a greater discussion with the toxic person once more. Keep in mind: You don't owe anybody a clarification. You can just gradually phantom out of their life to the degree essential, until you're never again influenced by the harmfulness That may appear glaringly evident, yet it very well may entice surmise that you need to make your removing clear and vocal, when in certainty the greater part of the work is your ally of the condition. Like a fire, you can just quit encouraging the flares.

Still, there's one specific scenario in which you might have to handle things a little differently: when toxic people are your blood relatives.

What to Do When a Toxic Person Is a Family Member

A toxic relative is a sticky situation. There are no easy answers and no standard answers that are right for everyone.

All things considered, removing toxic relatives may be the most essential cut you'll ever make. The family has a one of a kind method for getting under your skin and straightforwardly affecting your contemplations, practices, and decisions. Relatives don't possess you basically by being related by blood. Being family doesn't present any extraordinary exemptions to harmfulness. Relatives don't have a mysterious permit to botch your life. Keep in mind that.

Which is the reason basically making separation from toxic relatives is most likely the best move, regardless of whether it's physical or enthusiastic. Be that as it may, with regards to family (rather than companions or associates), your removing may require some extraordinary remittances. You may remove yourself inwardly, while as yet perceiving that you'll need to communicate with this person on a down to earth level (by observing them at occasion suppers, say, or dealing with a parent together). Without a doubt, your separating with a relative may expect you to unravel your functional inclusion from your passionate association — despite everything you'll consent to connect with this person when fundamental, however, you'll decline to give them a chance to drag you into the enthusiastic example of danger.

The imperative thing with family is to tread softly and make quiet, discerning choices since how you manage a harmful relative can shading your whole family relationship. There are regularly bigger expansive influences in a family than there are in a fellowship or working environment.

So ask yourself: What blowback will you get from other family members? What will the holidays be like? Can you realistically cut them out completely? You might answer these questions and still decide to separate yourself. Or you might modify your methodology as needs are. The critical thing is to set aside the opportunity to think about the dynamic and the impacts of the circumstance before choosing.

I won't lie: Cutting persons (particularly family) out of your life can be a standout amongst the most difficult things you can do. In any case, as we've stated, it's additionally a standout amongst the most freeing and groundbreaking choices you'll ever make.

Consider the study of Janice in our prologue, would she be happy having constant interactions with such a toxic person, despite her being the mother?

Above all, removing harmful persons sends a key message to yourself. You're stating: "I have esteem." You're organizing your joy over another person's brokenness. When you perceive how harmful persons can disintegrate this essential feeling of self-esteem, it winds up increasingly hard to permit them in your life.

Things You Can Learn From Toxic People

There's nothing you can learn from negative people, right? Not really.

For most of us, that's true--particularly because a bad attitude tends to rub off on everyone in the office. But you can also learn a few things about why people get angry, what makes them so miserable, and how to avoid some of the same pitfalls.

Before you try to "learn" from toxic people, guard yourself.

It's a trap that could bait you in. One day you are a cheerful representative, the following you are rounded with wrath and making sense of your leave system. From what we think about mind science, we as a whole have an inclination to harp on negative considerations and let them stew. They come less demanding to us, likely in light of the fact that it requires less exertion than really concocting arrangements.

Learn how to bounce away problems

Fundamentally, it's a method for managing pressure and negative contemplations. Simply throw them away quickly and consider different subjects. Toxic people don't bother. Hence they never try to figure out why. They don't bob anything. Actually, every remark, sideways look, and negative experience appears to stick to them and make a dull cloud. You can watch this occur continuously. A contrary person appears to nearly ache for toxic quality. They are a wipe for it, and they appear to be defenseless to the cloud framing. My recommendation: Bounce those contemplations away instantly.

Avoid "something better" syndrome

Toxic persons are continually looking at "something better" in work and life. They have a tendency to be bad-tempered and restless in light of the fact that whatever they are encountering now isn't sufficient. Only little measurements of introduction to this can be savage, so once you see it at work, try to maintain a strategic distance from this sort of reasoning however much as could reasonably be expected. The genuine truth? You don't know whether there is a superior work environment, or a superior employment, or a superior supervisor. In truth, you might be in a workplace that is harmful and you have to leave, yet for a large portion of us, you are most likely in a sensibly solid working environment - you accepted the position with high expectations, and it is anything but an awful technique to continue having those high expectations. For reasons unknown, toxic persons dependably figure "the following thing" will be better, regardless of what it is. More than anything, that makes a miserable presence.

Pay attention to who is investing in you

Another intriguing quality with all toxic persons is that they tend to move in packs. The harmful cloud extends, hooks onto another person, and structures a dim bond. Terrible organization adulterates, as is commonly said, and it likewise makes you hopeless. When you see a gathering of grumblers, take one moment to consider your identity around the most. My recommendation is to pick persons who will put resources into you, who need to see you develop and improve as a person. There's no harmful slop within these people; they won't destroy you with cynicism and sharpness. Look out for persons who have an understanding and an uplifting viewpoint. On the off chance that you are encompassed by hopeless persons, there's a decent shot you're going to wind up being hopeless too.

Epilogue

Do you have toxic people in your life?

Draining, non-supportive, and difficult people are one of life's greatest challenges.

You deserve to have people in your life who you enjoy spending time with, who support you, and who you love hanging out with.

All things considered, this book is implied as a general outline: Relationships are perplexing and it may not be anything but difficult to manage harmful persons until the point that you have gained from past cooperations. I comprehend that numerous connections, particularly familial ones, are more troublesome on the grounds that it's not all that simple to close the entryway and say farewell. In any case, most importantly on the off chance that you feel terrible about yourself because of an association with someone else, it's an ideal opportunity to take a seat and evaluate the issue. They might be probably not going to change, however, you can. Measure the experts (if there are any) and the cons, settle on a choice to confine your chance with this person or end the relationship—and don't think back.

Try not to enable yourself to end up drained because of giving and giving and receiving nothing consequently. At first, you may feel for them and their predicament however once you see that each cooperation is adversely charged you might need to restrain your contact with them, or possibly cut ties. Your chance and vitality are basic for your own particular life. Try not to be excessively eager to give them away.

All the best.